WIZARDS

OF ICE!

AF565509

POOJA SHEKHAR

Copyright © Pooja Shekhar
All Rights Reserved.

This book has been published with all efforts taken to make the material error-free after the consent of the author. However, the author and the publisher do not assume and hereby disclaim any liability to any party for any loss, damage, or disruption caused by errors or omissions, whether such errors or omissions result from negligence, accident, or any other cause.

While every effort has been made to avoid any mistake or omission, this publication is being sold on the condition and understanding that neither the author nor the publishers or printers would be liable in any manner to any person by reason of any mistake or omission in this publication or for any action taken or omitted to be taken or advice rendered or accepted on the basis of this work. For any defect in printing or binding the publishers will be liable only to replace the defective copy by another copy of this work then available.

Contents

Contents

1. Love Yourself

Love who you are
Love what you want to be
Love everything that's lost
Love everything that you have
Love everything about you

Loving oneself is the greatest pleasure of times
Loving oneself is the epitome of wholesomeness
Loving oneself can never go wrong
Loving oneself can never be lost

Waiting for others
Needing others
Depending on others needlessly
Love changes the definition

When one's in love
They fall in love with themselves
Whether it's someone else loving you
Or you yourself
So let's fall in love with ourselves first

2. Souls Apart

In another dimension
On another planet
How far have you gone
For me to reach you

A crack through which our souls can travel
In hopes of meeting one another someday
Experiencing heartbreak
Experiencing sadness
Of being apart

The souls cry in vain
The souls try in vain
In hopes of meeting another one day
Far away on unknown lands

3. History

Mornings bring hope
They bring a new life
Leaving behind yesterday
Making history

History that which lives
Lives on with us
Tormenting us
Encouraging us

To do better this day
To do better today
If not now
Then when will another history be made?

4. Dilemma

This world
This place
These people
Lost inside a dilemma

Scaling and judging
Deciding and following
Losing and finding
What doesn't exists

Imaginary are those rules
That have become real
Beliefs more powerful than reality
Twisting and turning it

Change the only constant
Nature decided by humans
Calling the artificial
The natural

5. He

This world sees
The one side of coins
The other side gets lost
From the worlds view

It's easy to forget
There's no need to remember
When something is alright
When someone is strong

The world rather would prefer
Being blind
To the mistakes of this world
If they were to the strong

There's no need he is strong
He is a man
Don't worry he'll handle things by himself
Rather than seeing the reality of the world

6. Words

This road will lead to nowhere
This path you should just give up
This world won't bow down to your wishes
These were the words

Of people
Of friends
Of family
But of not my soul

It burnt
To make the dreams come true
It believe in making a mere fantasy real
It wanted to know what it feels like

This road I kept on walking
This path I would always choose
I would bow down to my wishes
And choose the right words for myself

7. Hope

Hope
The only light in the darkness
Hope
The only path through the sadness

A mere emotion
Turning worlds upside down
Sometimes for the better
Sometimes for the worse

Hope can't be discarded
It is the fire that burns
Every moment of our lives
Giving us a fighting chance
To live by

Hope fills the existence
Of beings
Of success
Of stories
Of life

8. Complex Words

Why do I find them complex
And yet easy
When spoken they become cruel
When written they become friendly

Do I not know how to speak
Do I only know how to write
Does the disappointment only occurs when I speak
Does the might only shows when I write

This world is soulless
Without words
Being written and spoken
They're the colours of this black and white life
They're the souls of this soulless world

9. Be Me

There was no place
There were no people
Who could see the sparkle
Who could see the light

When time came
When it all became visible
People started to notice
And now
they wanted to be me

10. The City

They saw with pity
They saw with lust
They defiled others
At their own leisure

People forgot humanity
They lost their sanity
Sympathy was nowhere to be seen
Feelings were weighted on bounds

This was the pity
This was the city
The city of leisure
The city of seizure

11. Bounds

This world is bound
Bound to lust
Bound to hate
Bound to boundaries

Limitations is all it seeks
Limitations is all it reeks
Exercises it's limitations
Through humiliation

Defiling
Devouring
Like monsters
Like wild beasts

12. Colors

Black and White
Colourful and play
There's no grey
This is world is Gay

The colours life brings us
And the colours we offer to life
If not the same
Then similar as twins

So complex
And yet so easy
To understand humanity
To understand life

Cause the colours are either
Black and White
Or Colourful and play

13. Broken Feelings

Broken Feelings

Those feelings welling up inside of me
Those moments my heart was pierced
With pain and agony
When I saw you leave

In distance we saw each other
You appeared as a gleaming light
Fading slowly
As each minute passes by

It broke my heart
Leaving me in pain
It made me weep
It made me fade

Something lost
Which could never be found
Till time's end
I could never feel again

14. Best Friends

We started as strangers
We looked at each other
With wondering suspicious gazes
Then we smiled

It all started with a smile
Two strangers became friends
Suspicious gazes turned into loving gazes
With time we grew

Saw each other at their worst
Saw each other at their best
We passed through life
Holding onto each other
As best friends are supposed to do

15. Friend

It was a world where we didn't belong
It was a world where we couldn't belong
Black sheeps, outcasts
Call it whatever you want

But we found a place
Where we fit perfectly
With each other
Being a halves of the broken people we were

Together we came long
Made a world of our own
Together we built a world
Where everyone belonged
A place where everyone was each other's friend

16. Journey

A safe place
The journey of life
Became so great
With friends on our sides

Up and downs
Left and right
The time we spent together
Turned into adventures

With no one in sight
We still knew
There were people
Fond of us
Waiting at the end
End of the road

17. Societal Strength

It's childish they say
It's a sign of weakness they say
They say never to cry
They say never to bow

As strength lies
In the ones who never cry
In the ones who never bow
To anyone even themselves

The true definition is lost
With time and with society
The definition now has become
Artificial and a composition of society's idealism

18. Lio

A lion is a symbol
Of strength
Of vigour
He is the king

Of his kingdom
The ruler of the forest
The head of his family
The main hunter

The bread winner
The lion never gets tired
Never gives up
Always keeps going
With a golden heart

19. The Economy Of Humanity

This world shall know the truth
But on what price
A price which they wouldn't pay
A price after receiving they wouldn't care

The price of truth
Or the truth of survival
It's either of the two
The price of being alive in this world

Humanity generates economy
Economy generates insanity
Human's have lost their humanity
And have increased their economy

20. Champion

She endured through time
She endured through life
Mere surviving
Somehow she endured to live

Hurting in vain
Crying in pain
She felt as though
She was the only one for herself

True she knew how this world is
True she made it through
She felt like a champion
Standing in a crowd
With no audience to cheer her by

21. Oh I Wish!

Oh I wish! I could tell this world
To mind it's own business
And pay attention only to me
This world

Oh I wish! I could mourn the loss
Of something which I never had
Oh I wish I could tell this world
How much I hate it
While loving every bit and pieces of it

Oh I wish! I could tell this world
I love the fragrances of flowers
I love the sounds of rain
Thunder scares me
And sunrise calms me

But it shall never know
Since it has been negligent
Negligent in thinking about anything
Anything but me

22. World Of Tomorrow

World of Tomorrow
No one knows what is it
Or who it is
Since the places will change
The people will change
Or will they remain the same?
The places looking as though they were trapped in time
The faces looking as though they were trapped in picture

Wondering about the world of Tomorrow
We will someday die
Even after seeing tomorrows
Till the the day we die

23. Psychology The Only Biology

Good luck with your art
Good luck with your science
Good luck with your technology
Good luck with your biology

Your psychology
Not your priority
Not your individuality
Not your sincerity

Art is the world's soul
Science is the world's pillars
Technology is the world's growth
Biology is the world itself

But psychology is the only difference
The difference of inference
Without being evident
Evident to be true
Evident to be false

Evident to be precise
Evident to be vague

To be all and nothing at all

24. No Matter The World

Soon the sun will rise
Soon the we'll get the prize
Of being young
Of being sung

About the sorrow
You held inside
About the worries
That die deep inside

Leaving you soulless
Leaving you worthless
Of not being in this world
Of being
Being who you are
No matter the world

25. Bias

When I saw you
It made my heart break
Into pieces as I knew
Knew your feelings were same as mine

Knew the truth lying deep inside
Resulting in and anger
Since you couldn't show
The truth outside

The bias of this society
The worries of reputation
But why your worries were only about you
And I didn't exist

In this society of yours

26. Illusion

You shined bright
Like the sun
Lighting this world
Warmth of kindness

Pleasant sorrows
Sorrowful happy moments
Pain without any regrets
Regrets filled with happiness

This was our love
Something which existed
But could never become real
Cause reality is the ultimate illusion

27. Change

Change
Do we really need it?
Do we really need to be someone else?
Do we really need to follow someone else?

Being who we are
Right or wrong
God sees all
He gives us lessons
In ways we cannot fathom

Do not follow the rules made by humans
It is upon their own preferences
They created the rules
Profitable to the wealthy
Profitable to the powerful

28. Be Better

Be better
Be good
Do more
These were the lines
We heard the most

From the world
Which can't be better
Which can't be good
Which can't do more
Only to burden others in their stead

Follow rules
Making no sense
Follow others
Failing at every step

29. Humanity

I see the place
where I want to be
I know the place
where I am supposed to be

I know the world
Where I belong
I know the people
Where everyone loves

And it's my dream
To be a part of it
To be there
With the people I love
And the people who worship not gods
But humanity itself

30. Dreamworld

Why is it so hard
For people to dream
Of a world
Soo pure
Not petty
Lovely
Not ugly

And to follow through
And make their dreams come true
Why is it everyone wants
What they can't have
Because they don't want to be tired
Because they don't want to be fired

Creating the dreamworld
People lack dedication
Blaming their failures on others
Unwilling to leave this world
And live in their Dreamworld

31. Radha

Was it Radha's love?
Or her dedication to Krishna?
Or was it both?
That still wins the heart of millions

To be a tale of love like no other
Can never be found again through times
Unless a reincarnation of
Radha herself

Love of Radha
Won the hearts of people
And of Krishna himself
A tale we all know
That need not be told again
Still told a million times
To billions
Because a tale like this
Can never be re-written again

32. The Art Of Love

The art of love!
No one has mastered it
There's no curriculum to follow
There's no method we know of

The mystery of the world
The history of the world
The outcome of every interaction
The outcome of every intervention

Only if humans had mastered
The art of love
The world would've been different
The histories we know of
Would've changed

To what we do not know of
But we can fathom
How things would be

33. White

The colour of peace
The colour of tranquility
White as we know
Brings harmony

The world lays divided in different shades of colours
But comes United under one colour
The colour white
A symbol of peace
Of hope,of harmony

White is plain
And be painted red
Any colour we want
Any colour we desire
That's why it's important to be white
To be free of all colours and creeds

34. Shiva

They say he's the almighty
They say he's the all righty
The mightiest God to be worshipped
The first man ever existed

Declination in humanity
Resulted in insanity
The children of gods became humans
And humans became demons

Still they weren't lost
Cause Shiva never denied being worshipped
By humans or by demons
Cause he is the forefather of Humanity
Someone who doesn't know insanity
A god in the form of humans
A lord in the name of earth

9 798886 847512

Printed by Libri Plureos GmbH in Hamburg, Germany